Feng Shui

FOR THE HOME

A PRACTICAL AND EASY TO USE GUIDE
TO THE ART OF FENG SHUI IN THE HOME

Sasha Fenton

Published in the United Kingdom in 2000 by Caxton Editions
20 Bloomsbury Street
London WC1B 3QA
a member of the Caxton Publishing Group

© Copyright 2000 Caxton Publishing Group

Designed and Produced for Caxton Editions by Open Door Limited
80 High Street, Colsterworth, Lincolnshire, NG33 5JA
Illustration: Andrew Shepherd, Art Angle
Colour separation: GA Graphics Stamford

Title: Feng Shui, For the Home
ISBN: 1-84067-236-6

Picture credits
PhotoDisc images: 10, 12, 14, 16, 18, 23, 24, 26, 28, 30, 34, 36, 37, 38, 39, 54, 55, 56, 57, 58,
59, 60, 66, 68, 69, 70, 71, 72, 74, 75, 76, 78, 80, 81, 82, 83, 84, 86, 88, 89, 90, 91, 92, 94

Feng Shui

FOR THE HOME

Sasha Fenton

CAXTON EDITIONS

Contents

Contents

Feng Shui

The name "Feng Shui" means wind and water. This may sound like a medical condition but wind and water are the elemental energies that are associated with two of the trigrams of the I Ching.

Trigram Sun – *which rules wind*

Trigram Tui – *which rules "lake" or water*

It is interesting to see that both these trigrams have the same pattern but in a reverse configuration to each other.

Feng Shui itself is the art of direction and placement. British astrologer, Russell Grant, and others have popularised Feng Shui through the medium of the television and they have taught the British to pronounce this Foong Shway. I have lived and worked in China and become familiar with the pronunciation, Fungshoi or even Fungsoi with the "ung" bit said in the way that a Londoner would say "bung", and to me it will always be Fungshoi. However, China is a big place and the same words are pronounced differently in different places, so however you choose to pronounce this will be right somewhere in the Middle Kingdom!

The roots of modern Feng Shui are an ancient mix of geomancy (reading or divining the earth), astrology, numerology, compass reading, myth and encouraging the right kind of spiritual or ghostly help. Also included in this melee are the I Ching, the Lo Shu and man's natural desire to feel safe in his own home. The Chinese have been practising Feng Shui for centuries and despite being banned by their Communist government, they still practice it today. It only reached the west to any great extent within the last ten years when business people in the City of London started to copy the style of the highly successful business houses in Hong Kong and Singapore. After entering western minds and hearts through the avenue of the business community Feng Shui is now extremely popular. There are people who make a great deal of money by advising business houses but it is perfectly possible to obtain Feng Shui advice for your own home for no more than the price of this book.

I myself recently noticed the effects of Feng Shui in a quite dramatic manner when I was recently asked to give a talk at a bookshop in central London. The shop manager had thoughtfully given me a space that was in a nicely tucked away part of the shop. A few rows of seats were placed in front of me, and behind the seats was an

escalator bringing people directly up from the floor below. The talk progressed well, but a number of people got up and left. I noticed that the first to go were those in the back row directly in front of the "mouth" of the escalator. Then the couple who had been sitting immediately in front of them got up and left and so on, until there was a completely clear corridor running one-seat-behind-the-other from front to back. As more people arrived, I asked them not to sit in this "corridor" area but to grab a spare seat and move it to the side. Nobody else drifted away after that.

A Short History of Feng Shu

Feng Shui is not a stand-alone system but part of a group of interrelated Chinese divinations that include the I Ching, Chinese astrology and the Lo Shu, which is more commonly known by the Japanese name of Nine Star Ki.

The I Ching

The earliest from of recorded divination in China (and possibly in the world), is the I Ching, and an early form of this was used by pre-historic tribes in China possibly as far back as the end of the last ice age. This very basic form of divination was achieved by examining cracks in the burned shoulder blade bones of sheep or goats. The Chinese believed that a crack that formed an unbroken line was Yang or yes, while a broken line was Yin or no. These ancient people believed that this yes/no form of guidance was sent by the gods (or by their ancestors) to guide them when making important decisions.

An Emperor called Fu Hsi is credited with many early divination discoveries. On one occasion, Fu Hsi was taking a walk by the banks of a river when he saw a fabulous animal called a hippogriffin climbing out of a river. This animal was probably one of the small, shy pre-historic Mongolian horses that still exist in small pockets in northern areas and which had strayed south during or after a cold winter. This horse has vague zebra-like lines on the flanks of its rump. Emperor Fu Hsi, who lived 3,000 BC, is said to have discovered the three lined trigrams of the I Ching in the markings on the horse's side. The I Ching trigrams passed down both verbally at first, and later by being burned into strips of bamboo. In the 12th century BC, King Wen wrote the first commentaries on the trigrams. Later on Tan, the son of King Wen, along with the Duke of Chou continued to work on the I Ching. The Duke of Chou is credited with being the one who had the idea of piling one atop the other in order to create the famous hexagrams. A famous scholar who lived much later and who added commentaries to the I Ching was no other than Confucius.

The Lo Shu (also known as Nine Star Ki)

Many early peoples believed that gods live on mountain tops but the ancient Chinese believed that gods and deities lived in rivers. One day, while out walking, Emperor Fu Hsi (the same chap who spotted the Hippogriffin and invented the I Ching), saw a magical turtle climbing out of a river. Turtles have always been revered in China due to their much envied longevity, so they already qualified as a kind of godly or mythical animal before anything else was added to them.

Fu Hsi noticed a particularly regular square pattern of nine squares on the creature's back. With a flash of insight worthy of Archimedes, Fu Hsi is said to have worked out that when the numbers one to nine were placed in a particular pattern in the square, they came to fifteen whichever direction they were added up in. Later, this magic square became attached to Feng Shui, as we will soon see.

Right: the magical turtle with nine squares on its back.

Below: the Lo Shu, also known as the Nine star Ki and the magic square.

4	9	2
3	5	7
8	1	6

Another possible root of the Lo Shu is based on an ancient form of astronomy and astrology. This early form of astrology was very different from the kind that we know in the west. Our astrology is based upon the constellations that lie along the apparent path of the sun, while the Lo Shu (or Nine Star Ki) is based on the seven stars of the Little Bear, in addition to the Pole Star and Vega.

After a long period of instability in China, strong government was imposed by the Emperor Chin. This tough-guy banned books in an effort to control the minds of his subjects. Many early myths and divination systems must have perished but some survived, carried by word of mouth and by the Gypsies. Some sources suggest that the I Ching was never completely banned but studying the stars for divination purposes certainly was – and it stayed that way for some centuries. This lead to a shift from the stellar roots of the system to the calendar and numeric systems that are in use today in such divinations as Chinese astrology, the Four Pillars of Destiny, the Lo Shu and Feng Shui, which is a spin-off from all the other divinations.

The I Ching is a form of philosophy and fortune telling, while the Lo Shu and astrology are used for character reading and predicting events; the Feng Shui is the directional branch of these systems, and it has been permeated with ideas from geomancy, myth, spirituality and legend.

Yang and Yin

No book on Chinese divination would be complete without an explanation of these two forces. Yang is the positive, masculine, aggressive force that gets things done but which can go over the top and become destructive. Yin is the negative, feminine, passive/receptive force that endures, nurtures and conserves, but it can become ossified and unable to move with the times. The Chinese believe that both forces are necessary in nature and in life and that a balance of Yang and Yin are needed. I have rarely found this adequately explained in terms of Feng Shui, except in highly complex levels of Chinese numerical divination, so I have only alluded to it where absolute necessary in this book.

Good Chi circulates gently around an area, while bad Chi either forces itself into an area like an imaginary wind or it stagnates in a dead corner like a murky pool. Long before Feng Shui became popular, I learned from the Chinese themselves that they believe bad spirits travel in straight lines while good ones wander about in a swaying fashion. It is this belief that is brought into the sections in books such as this when we discuss front paths and hallways inside our houses.

The Pa Kua (sometimes spelled Ba Gua) is the familiar eight sided figure that appears in every book on Feng Shui. This usually has a mirror in the middle and the eight trigrams of the I Ching arranged around the sides of the Pa Kua. You can pick up a Pa Kua in any new age shop, in any Chinatown around the world and in many gift shops.

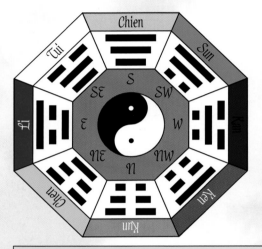 

Above: the Pa Kua of Early Heaven (left) used in mainly in Feng Shui around the tombs and graves of ancestors. The Pa Kua of the Later Heaven (right) appears to be more significant to dwelling places and so more appropriate for what we are trying to achieve in this book.

Some Feng Shui practitioners suggest that you hang an early heaven arrangement Pa Kua in your window or front door to reflect evil influences away from the house, as this Pa Kua is protective. It would be well worth putting up a Pa Kua if your home fronts on to something unpleasant, but a polished convex brass plaque would do just as well. As it happens, I am writing this book in the midst of a move of house and I have just discovered that the back of my house faces a dock which has the heaviest crane in Europe clearly visible, and I have been told that this crane actually lifts nuclear submarines and nuclear missiles in and out of the water. I think that a brass plaque and probably a huge Pa Kua will be the first thing I fit there.

The Pa Kua and the I Ching

The eight trigrams of the I Ching are arranged around the eight sides of the Pa Kua. The trigrams of the I Ching take eight forms, ranging from three unbroken Yang lines through every variation to three broken Yin lines. Each of these has a meaning and each has two popular names, one of which relates to a geographical or meteorological feature and another that relates to a family member. Each trigram also relates to a direction, a colour and a season (among many other things). The directions link up exactly with those of the Magic Square, so the Pa Kua can be used in its place. When you look at the Pa Kua and the Magic square together you can see the connection. The Pa Kua has eight sides and a centre, while the Magic square has eight sides and a central number.

Chien

Trigram name:	heaven
Family member:	father
Season:	late autumn
Direction:	northwest
Element:	big metal

Kun

Trigram name:	earth
Family member:	mother
Season:	late summer-early autumn
Direction:	southwest
Element:	big earth

Chen

Trigram name:	thunder
Family member:	eldest son
Season:	spring
Direction:	east
Element:	big wood

Kan

Trigram name:	WATER
Family member:	MIDDLE SON
Season:	WINTER
Direction:	NORTH
Element:	WATER

Ken

Trigram name:	MOUNTAIN
Family member:	YOUNGEST SON
Season early:	SPRING
Direction:	NORTHEAST
Element:	SMALL EARTH

Sun

Trigram name:	WIND (ALSO WOOD)
Family member:	ELDEST DAUGHTER
Season:	EARLY SUMMER
Direction:	SOUTHEAST
Element:	SMALL WOOD

Li

Trigram name:	fire
Family member:	middle daughter
Season:	summer
Direction:	south
Element:	fire

Tui

Trigram name:	Lake
Family member:	youngest daughter
Season:	autumn
Direction:	west
Element:	small metal

You may wonder why I have included such arcane matters as family members in this book but the Chinese actually call the trigrams "Mother", "Youngest Son" etc. The names, Heaven, Thunder, Lake give a clue to the character of each trigram and they can suggest geographic locations or directions that are beneficial for one thing or another. The seasons are worth including as there might be a time of the year in which you use some parts of a house in preference to others (e.g. the fireplace in winter, the garden in summer).

The elements

The elements come into every branch of Chinese divination and they are supremely important when it comes to Feng Shui. In Chinese astrology, these are called the Heavenly Stems. The familiar Chinese zodiac signs of the Rat, Ox, Tiger etc. are called the Earthly Branches. Four of the elements are attached to the four points of the compass, with the fifth element representing the centre. I have mentioned colours, directions and seasons here and there in this book but I haven't strongly suggested that an ornament in the shape of a dragon, turtle, tiger or phoenix be used on or in a house. If you wish to do so, ensure that these animals are in the right part of the house and the right part of a room.

Green Dragon

Element name:	*wood*
Direction:	*east*
Season:	*spring*
Colour	*green*
Animal:	*dragon*

Red Phoenix

Element name:	fire
Direction:	south
Season:	summer
Colour:	red
Animal:	phoenix

The Emperor

Element name:	earth
Direction:	centre
Season:	mid-seasons
Colour:	yellow
Animal:	emperor

The White Tiger

Element name:	metal
Direction:	west
Season:	autumn
Colour:	white
Animal:	tiger

The Black Turtle

Element name:	water
Direction:	north
Season:	winter
Colour:	black/blue
Animal:	turtle

Choosing a Property

So you've won a pile of money or inherited a fortune and you can afford to build your perfect home and now you can really get down to some serious consideration of Feng Shui. The most propitious arrangement is to build your house facing more or less towards the south (the red phoenix) which should have small mound or hills in the landscape and a river meandering through it, with mountains or high buildings behind the house to the north (the black turtle). The land to the west should have hills (the white tiger) and to the east there should be slightly higher hills (the green dragon).

NB: If you live in the southern hemisphere, swap these directions around.

If you are deeply into Chinese astrology and you happen to know which of the five elements features most strongly on your Chinese horoscope chart, you can choose a house that is built with the right materials for your horoscope.

Wood: wooden cladding.

Fire: brick.

Earth: stone.

Metal: white texture or stone country house.

Water: a house on the edge of the sea or a lake.

The chances are that such a dream house is beyond you, so let us take a look at what you might reasonably choose if you happen to be looking for a new address.

The Chinese hate the winter when nothing grows and when the weather can be very cold indeed, so like the Vikings they associate the north with bad things. Chinese homes were traditionally built around an open front courtyard and the dust and heat of summer could be sucked into the courtyards and open front of the house. This means that they preferred not to position the house directly towards the south. Probably the best direction of all is south east where the sun shines most of the day but eases off in the later afternoon. The house should not have rising ground at the front but it should face downhill.

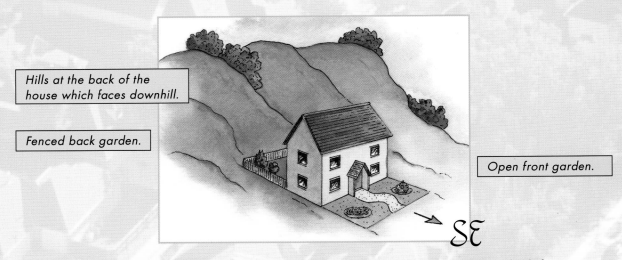

Hills at the back of the house which faces downhill.

Fenced back garden.

Open front garden.

Another early consideration was that of safety, and while a stockade or high fence might be erected at the back of the property the undefended open courtyard area at the front should have a good view of approaching enemies or of honoured visitors on their way to the house.

Rivers and roads

Rivers were the roads of ancient China so both rivers and roads are looked at in a similar way in Feng Shui. It is best to avoid having a river or road to the back of your property, especially if the water (or traffic) is fast flowing as this will cause feelings restlessness and insecurity and it's energy could wash your money away. I have actually lived in a place that had a fast flowing river at its back, and however hard I worked and however much I tried to save, I couldn't hang on to money there. A river in the front or on either side of the house is fine, as long as it bends and doesn't flow too quickly. A main road is considered much the same as a river, so if you must live directly on a street with no front garden between you and the roadway, then try to make this a side street.

What is Chi?

If you find yourself getting interested in Oriental forms of divination, you will come across this word in a variety of different spellings and pronunciations such as Ki, Kee, Qi but the usual pronunciation in the west is Chi as in the popular exercise regime, Tai Chi.

Chi simply means energy, in this case a form of psychic energy of the kind that we understand as good or bad vibes. We all know what it feels like when someone takes an irrational dislike to us and sends us bad vibes and there are many people who refuse to purchase a house on the basis that they don't like its vibrations. The Chinese don't wait to feel these vibes, they know how Chi travels and they do their best to encourage beneficial Chi and to discourage unfavourable Chi. Good Chi circulates gently around an area, while bad Chi either forces itself into an area like an imaginary wind or it stagnates in a dead corner like a murky pool. Long before Feng Shui became popular, I learned from the Chinese themselves that they believe bad spirits travel in straight lines while good ones wander about in a swaying fashion. This means that the kind of straight front path beloved of Victorian builders encourages bad Chi, while a wandering front path encourages good Chi. We will come back to this again shortly when we look at front doors and passages within a house.

Feng Shui advises against living opposite a fork in a river where the point of land that is created by the fork points directly towards the house or within a fork in the river. There are two problems here, one is that a fork that points towards a house

The fork in the river will shoot negative Chi into the house.

The vortex of the rivers meeting produces restless and uncomfortable Chi energy.

forms an arrow that can shoot negative Chi into the house, while being within a fork is too near to the vortex that is created by the meeting of two sources of water. This vortex brings a restless and uncomfortable form of Chi energy.

Living by a stream or river may be common in some rural areas and in wet parts of the world such as Florida in the USA, but urban settings, it is the presence of roads that require attention. The worst case scenario is a house that faces a T Junction where the traffic comes directly towards the house. If this is a one-way-street, it is just about acceptable if traffic moves away from the house, but no good at all if it flows directly towards it. The only way around this problem (apart from moving) is to close off the front door and use a side door, while filling the front garden with fluffy bushes and hedges that cut off the flow of Chi.

Traffic flowing directly towards a house opposite a T-junction brings fast flowing Chi straight into the house.

Closing off the front door and planting fluffy bushes in the front garden will help to cut off the flow of Chi.

If the house is bounded by a river on one side and a road on the other, try to locate the front door so that it faces the river. Much the same goes for a house with a front door facing high ground. In this case, close off the front door and make another entrance somewhere else.

When a house has a river one side and a road the other, try to locate the front door facing the river.

People in cities quite like living on a corner as they don't feel as hemmed in by other buildings as they would in the middle of a row of houses, but a busy corner is not considered to be a wonderful location by the rules of Feng Shui. This arrangement brings the Chi traffic close to at least two sides of the building and the building diagonally opposing the property will throw "secret arrows" straight towards it.

Nobody would choose to live by a cemetery or a rubbish dump and the Chinese would definitely avoid such places. Homes built on ancient burial sites should also be avoided as they are considered to be unlucky and also a constant reminder of death. It would be nice to live without a view of the gasworks or the local tanning factory and the Chinese would be the first to agree. Of course, we all have to cut our coats according to the cloth that we can afford, but if you are moving house try to keep some of the above considerations in mind before you purchase.

House numbers

There are many people in the western world who refuse to buy a house with the number 13. There are buildings and hotels that don't use the number 13 for floors or rooms and aeroplanes which don't have a number 13 row of seats. The root of this superstition comes from the last supper where thirteen sat down to eat.

Some Chinese are fussy about numbers and you may come across books that tell you that they hate the number four because it sound like the Chinese word si, which means death. Before you start worrying about this, bear in mind that China is a large country and that there are many Chinese languages, also it is mainly the Cantonese from the south whose culture has reached the west. Other parts of China have different likes and dislikes and many northern Chinese are less bothered by numerology.

Numbers

For those of you who want to take an interest in the Chinese view of house numbers, the following list shows the supposedly lucky and unlucky ones.

2	*Two indicates easy achievement and happiness.*
22	*Twenty-two indicates double happiness.*
5	*Five is linked to the five elements of Wood, Fire, Earth, Metal and Water.*
6	*Six symbolises wealth.*
8	*Eight brings great wealth.*
9	*Nine is associated with longevity.*

10	Ten denotes sureness or certainty.
1	The number one is considered to be unbalanced because it doesn't contain both Yang and Yin.
3	Three is liked by some Chinese and not by others.
4	Four sounds like the word "death" in Cantonese.

The Chinese don't contract numbers down to single digits in the way that western numerologists do, so twenty-two would not contract down to four (2 + 2 = 4). Each number is taken in its own right. For example, 28 is a wealth indicator, while 888 is a sure fire "get-rich-quick" number.

The way your house faces

Most people have a rough idea of the direction in which their property faces, even only to know where the sun shines at different hours of the day. As far as Feng Shui is concerned there are various ways of approaching the question of direction. One is to choose a direction that suits your particular purpose, another is to choose a direction that is generally liked by the Chinese, while the third is to choose one that links with one of your own lucky directions.

Let us look at the most practical option for a moment. An artist requires a north facing attic or conservatory with lots of light, while a keen gardener will want a garden that has a mixture of sun and shade. If you happen to spend a lot of time in the kitchen, you might like to have the sun there in the morning. The second option is to bear in mind that ancient Chinese houses had a courtyard and an open frontage, so they preferred these to face south east or perhaps south west, rather than towards the cold north winds. One thing that Feng Shui is fairly insistent upon is that a child's room should have a window that faces east, as this will benefit the child's health. But we will look at this more clearly when we look at individual rooms.

Your lucky direction

If you want to work out your lucky direction properly, you will need to consult an expert who also has great experience and knowledge of the complexities Chinese astrology and numerology. Such a person would use a Lo Pan, which is sometimes called the Chinese compass. The Lo Pan is used in conjunction with a magnetic compass, in addition to details of your personal horoscope, your personal numerology, the time of your life, the date when you purchase your new home and so on.

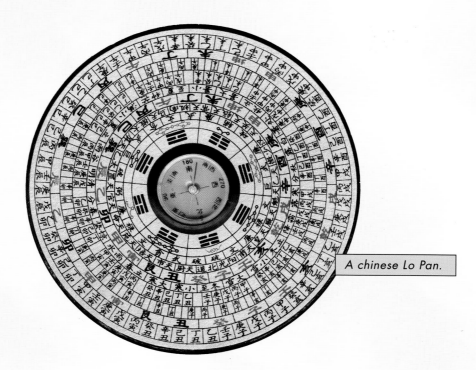

A chinese Lo Pan.

Your lucky number and directions

Now you can find the lucky number and the compass directions for your year of birth. As there are a number of directions that are fortunate for each person, with a bit of luck you will find at least one that fits one of your partner's lucky directions as well. While we are at it, we will take note of your lucky element, because you might find this piece of information handy when we start to look at each individual room within a house.

In the Year Number table below, find your year of birth and then track up to the top to find the lucky number for that year. For example, if you were born in 1975, the number in the top column is 7.

Year Numbers 1901-2017

9	8	7	6	5	4	3	2	1
1901	1902	1903	1904	1905	1906	1907	1908	1909
1910	1911	1912	1913	1914	1915	1916	1917	1918
1919	1920	1921	1922	1923	1924	1925	1926	1927
1929	1929	1930	1931	1932	1933	1934	1935	1936
1937	1938	1939	1940	1941	1942	1943	1944	1945
1946	1947	1948	1949	1950	1951	1952	1953	1954
1955	1956	1957	1958	1959	1960	1961	1962	1963
1964	1965	1966	1967	1968	1969	1970	1971	1972
1973	1974	1975	1976	1977	1978	1979	1980	1981
1982	1983	1984	1985	1986	1987	1988	1989	1990
1991	1992	1993	1994	1995	1996	1997	1998	1999
2000	2001	2002	2003	2004	2005	2006	2007	2008
2009	2010	2011	2012	2013	2014	2015	2016	2017

Locate your lucky number in the left hand column of the Lucky Direction table below and make a note of your lucky element and also your lucky directions. You will notice that there are two sets of directions for No. 5 (Earth) according to your gender. There are ancient reasons for this which are beyond the scope of this book. You may also notice that some of the directions double up for different numbers which share the same element. For instance, both 6 and 7 are Metal numbers so their directions are the same.

Armed with this information, you can either choose a house that faces the right way for yourself and your family, or if this is impossible you might choose to site important rooms in directions that suit each member of your family.

Lucky direction table

Lucky number	Element	Lucky directions
1	Water	East, North, West, N. West, S. East
2	Earth	West, South, S. West, N. West, S. East
3	Wood	East, S. East, North, South
4	Wood	East, S. East, North, South
5 (men)	Earth	West, South, S. West, N. West, S. East
5 (women)	Earth	West, N. West, S. West, North, N. East
6	Metal	West, N. West, S. West, North, N. East
7	Metal	West, N. West, S. West, North, N. East
8	Earth	West, South, S. West, N. West, S. East
9	Fire	East, South, S. East, S. West, N. East

If the house direction is absolutely no good for you or any of your loved ones, you can redeem the situation. You can paint the house or some part of the house a colour that fits with your lucky number element. The most important and the easiest thing that you can do to bring luck your way is to choose the right colour for your front door. In addition, you can use a particular material on your door on some kind of decoration that is fixed to the front of the house in order to improve your luck. Take a look at the companion book to this one which is all about Feng Shui for the garden, because there you will notice that you can plant certain trees and flowers or choose the right colours that will enhance or improve your luck in the all important front area of your house.

fix some kind of decoration to the front of your house or door.

paint the house or door a colour that fits your lucky number.

choose the right colour and material for your front door.

choose plants and flowers which will enhance your luck in your front garden.

Lucky number	Element	Luck changers
1	Water	Woodwork or front door in black or dark blue. Watery coloured stained glass. Put a little stone turtle in front garden.
2	Earth	Woodwork or front door in yellow. Chinese emperor picture or statuette in hallway.
3	Wood	Natural woodwork or green paint. Bushes in front garden. Decorative dragon doorknob or fixture.
4	Wood	Natural woodwork or green paint. Bushes in front garden. Decorative dragon doorknob or fixture.
5 (men)	Earth	Woodwork or front door in yellow. Chinese emperor picture or statuette in hallway.
5 (women)	Earth	Woodwork or front door in yellow. Chinese emperor picture or statuette in hallway.
6	Metal	White woodwork or door. Decorative tiger fixture or picture of tiger inside the hallway.
7	Metal	White woodwork or door. Decorative tiger fixture or picture of tiger inside the hallway.
8	Earth	Woodwork or front door in yellow. Yellow flowers in front garden. Chinese emperor picture or statuette in hallway.
9	Fire	Woodwork or front door in red. Image of a bird in stained glass or as decorative fixture or as a picture inside the hallway.

The Outside of Your Property

From this point onwards, we take a look not only at new property but also at potential problems regarding the outside of an existing one and what can be done to alleviate them.

A little earlier in this book, I mentioned the subject of Chi and how the Chinese believe that bad Chi travels in straight lines. Nowadays it is more fashionable to say that straight lines encourage Chi to move too quickly rather than to suggest that it is good or bad. Either way, a straight front path leading to the door is not a great idea. It has become old fashioned to have a gate at the end of one's front path, but from the point of view of Feng Shui, this is a very good idea as it will slow down the flow of Chi from the street outside. If it is possible to break up the line of a straight path with a few bushes or pot plants, you should do so.

A gate at the end of your path leading to the front door will help slow down the flow of Chi from the outside street.

Break up the line of a straight path by planting bushes or placing pot plants along the path which will soften the edges.

A polished metal door knob or letterbox will help to fend off secret arrows.

A common problem that is easily dealt with is that of secret arrows. These aren't glares from unpleasant neighbours but invisible forces that shoot themselves directly towards the front of your home – and especially towards the vulnerable front door. A fence that points a sharp corner in the direction of the door or a square shaped lamp-post that points a corner to the door will shoot secret arrows towards it. A church or any old building that has gargoyles, devils or some other form of unpleasant statuary pointing to your door will need to be fended off. These problems are easily remedied by putting something reflective on the outer wall or on the front door. A polished metal letterbox or doorknob will help, as would fixing a symbol of a lucky dragon on to the wall. In both China and in the west a horseshoe is considered a lucky charm, so one of these can also be fixed over the door or on a nearby wall. Keep all such

A lucky dragon will fend off secret arrows.

metal objects clean or polished or they will lose their effectiveness. Some practitioners suggest that you hang a Pa Kua on the front of your house or that you have one facing out through a window.

keep metal object clean and shiny so that they remain effective guardians against secret arrows.

A Pa Kua's strong powers will ward off secret arrows if placed on your front door.

If you like the decorative stone lions that can be placed on a wall, these will certainly keep bad influences out of your home but they will drive them straight into the house opposite. For the sake of good neighbourliness, it might be better to do without these unless the front of your property faces open land. Even if you absolutely loathe the people who live opposite you, most magical systems the world over suggest that deliberately or knowingly sending bad luck will rebound three times on you, so don't do it!

The Layout of Your House

There are various ways of approaching this, so let us look them all.

Using a compass

You can use a compass to work out the direction that your property faces and then figure out which room aligns to which compass point - e.g. north, north east, north west, south and so on. If you are happy with this, you can simply go on to read the interpretations that appear a little later in this chapter because they are all marked with compass points. For example, if you look at the interpretation section called "Square one", you will see that it is sub-titled North.

The Magic Square

If you are not happy using a compass but you are artistic enough to sketch out a rough diagram of the layout of your property you should fit your diagram into the Magic Square as per the illustration on p. 41. Tradition says that you should include everything that is on your land, including the garden, outbuildings the farmyard and so on. However this is neither practical nor is it the way that Feng Shui is done these days, so just fit your house into the Magic Square and consult the companion book to this one for your garden or land.

Note: The Magic Square is called Magic because the numbers in it add up to 15 whether the calculation is done horizontally, vertically or diagonally.

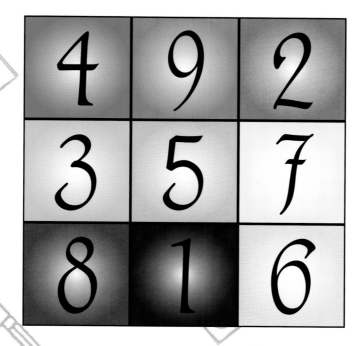

NB: If you have an enquiring mind you might find yourself wishing to link the numbers of the Magic Square with the compass directions that are mentioned in the interpretations. This can be done, but you have to turn the Magic Square 180 degrees so that what was up becomes down and what was left becomes right. The roots of this lie in ancient astronomy and astrology and oddly enough the same situation applies to western horoscope charts.

Place your diagram so that your front door or main entrance is aligned to the base of the Magic Square where the numbers 8,1,6 are located. Now look at each part of your house and read the interpretations.

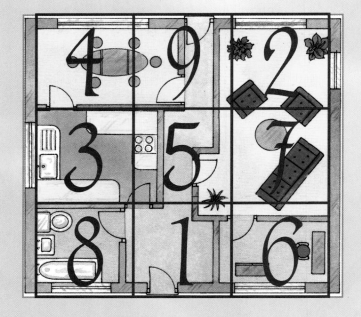

If your house is an irregular shape, don't leave any part of it hanging outside the square. This means that one or two parts of the square will be outside the boundaries of your house but for the moment, just make a note of any of these.

Each segment of the Magic Square relates to a different sphere of life, thus if area is missing you will lose out on the luck associated with that segment. The remedy is simple. Just place a mirror inside your house against the wall that abuts on to the missing area, as this will give an illusion of stretching the house outwards so that the missing bit is filled in.

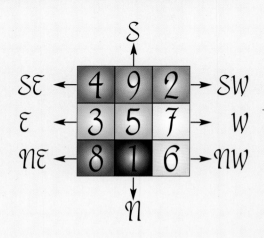

Squares within squares

Some people prefer to make diagrams while others have the kind of spatial mind that means that they can see things in their heads. If you are one of the spatial types, hold this book in your hand and face the directions that rule each sector of the Magic Square and then walk around your property looking at each room in turn.

Here is a quick list of the relevant directions.

There are two schools of thought as to how to use the directions and the magic square and you can try both. The first method is to always place the magic square over a diagram of your home with the numbers 8, 1 and 6 at the front of the house. In this case, you simply have to use the names of the directions as part of the mythology. For example, north having the attributes of spring growth. The second method is to turn the Magic Square to fit the actual directions in your home, so if your bedroom faces east, to put it there. The fact that north is at the bottom of the square and south at the top is a hang over from when the ancient astrological charts

Square Direction

Square one:	**north**
Square six:	**north west**
Square seven:	**west**
Square two:	**south west**
Square nine:	**south**
Square four:	**south east**
Square three:	**east**
Square eight:	**north east**

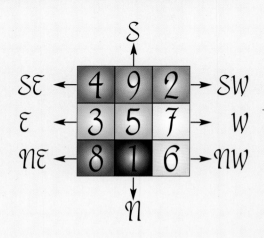

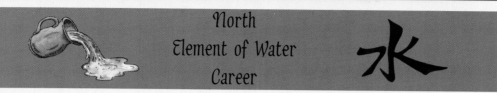

North
Element of Water
Career

水

The Chinese associate the flow of water with communications, and to their way of thinking this makes this part of the house especially important for career and business matters. If your career isn't flowing in the direction that you would like or if you can't earn any money from your work, put a water feature of some kind in this room. If you have ever wondered why so many Chinese restaurants and even take-out shops have fish tanks in them, now you know. The colours black or blue will help as would a picture of a river, a lake or a gentle seascape – with or without boats in it, but not a picture of a stormy sea or bad weather. If this area is missing from your home, hang a mirror on the wall to extend it. As soon as you improve this area you will notice an improvement in your level of intuition as well as in your career. If you leave the area unattended to for long enough, you will not only lose the capacity to earn money or to be intuitive but you will also begin to fall ill. A front door that faces directly north or that is in the middle of the front of the house will encourage success in career and business matters. If you wish to further enhance your career, paint your door black or dark blue.

nw

n

ne

4	9	2
3	5	7
8	1	6

South west
Element of Earth
Relationships

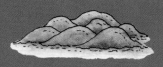

This Square concerns relationships of all kinds and especially love relationships and marriage. If this sector of your house is messy and muddled, your love life will become correspondingly messy. If you use this part of the house as a workshop, then either change things around or perhaps put a love nest in among the tools! If this area is missing from your house you may be able to put up a mirror to extend the house in this direction. If there is no practical way of changing rooms around or of putting up a mirror, wait until later in this book to see what you can do to enhance the rooms you use actually use for sleeping in or for sitting around in. You can use the Earth colour of yellow or shades of the Fire colours of red, pink or even purple on the walls or in your furnishings and accessories to improve this area of the house. This area could end up looking rather feminine, but so be it.

4	9	2
3	5	7
8	1	6

East
Element of Wood
Family

The Feng Shui concept in this sector of your house might be a difficult concept for westerners to understand but it makes perfect sense to the Chinese. This area refers to your ancestors, your family history and to the town or the home in which you grew up. The Chinese (and also the Africans) believe that if your dear departed ancestors are on your side you will receive their spiritual help, but if they are angry your luck will run out pretty damn quick. The family aspect to this square also relates to your current family, but it also refers to the group of people among whom you spend your working day or your social life – in short, a sort of extended family. Oddly enough, this is also considered to be an area of the house that brings life and energy. The desire for strong and healthy children means that this eastern direction is ideal for them to sleep in. A touch of green here and some green plants will do the world of good as will a wooden wall unit or cabinet. A dragon ornament or illustration and small pictures of your ancestors won't hurt either. If you enhance this area, you will notice an improvement in your family relationships (especially with the older generation) and you might even be able to look forward to an inheritance one of these days.

4	9	2
3	5	7
8	1	6

South east
Element of Wood
Wealth

This area relates to prosperity and wealth and if you allow it to become a mess then your wealth will suffer. Oddly enough you should choose to use some very bright coloured accessories here like purple, red and blue. Hanging some Chinese coins on the wall or placing some toy money on a shelf should help. If this part of the house happens to be the toilet or a corner that collects junk you will not only notice your money draining away but your health will also suffer. The remedy is to tidy the area and if it does happen to be the loo, to put a vigorous pot plant in here and the best choice would be a money plant. Another nice idea is to hang some of those toy Chinese coins up on a string or perhaps keep a jar of ordinary pennies, foreign coins or any other type of small denomination coins on a shelf.

4	9	2
3	5	7
8	1	6

The centre
The element of Earth
Health

To find the centre of your house, either draw or mentally mark out two diagonal lines that run from corner to corner of your property and then note where they cross. This is the health area of your home. For good health, this should be kept as clear as possible and not filled up with clutter. It is fine to have a coffee table here but clear dirty cups, old newspapers and other junk away as soon as you have finished with it all. This is also the area that blends the masculine and energetic force of Yang with the feminine and passive force of Yin. Keeping this area clean and clear will strike a good balance between these forces, and this will prevent you from feeling as though your life is either too hectic for comfort or too boring for words.

4	9	2
3	5	7
8	1	6

Square six

North west
The element of Metal
Travel, trade, friends, allies

This area of the house rules three quite different ideas. Like Square number three, it has a spiritual component in that it is thought to encourage beneficial gods and spirits into the home. The second issue is that this area is concerned with international trade and travel. The issue of international trade has far more importance when assessing a business than a private home, but who knows when you might want to buy or sell something over the Internet! Travel is of interest to many people nowadays and there is nothing worse than looking forward to a great holiday, only to have it spoiled by back luck. The other aspect of this area concerns neighbours, friends and allies. On the face of it, this may not appear as important to you as love or money but poor relationships with neighbours can be a nightmare, and without friends or allies life becomes very hard indeed. Colours that enhance this area are pale ones such as cream and white, while metallic ornaments, such as a metal table lamp with a cream shade will bring good luck.

4	9	2
3	5	7
8	1	6

West
The element of Metal
Creativity, fertility, children

Like the previous square this is also associated with friends, but less in the form of the support or alliances than social life and the fun you have with your pals. Creativity encompasses any form of creation, so business projects or hobbies can be included here as well as painting the odd masterpiece or two. Being a Metal area, the best colours are light ones, especially white and cream, and it helps to have pleasant paintings ornaments or a valued gift displayed here. If you want to start a family or to have happy and healthy children, you must look after this area and keep unpleasant or dirty objects out of it.

4	9	2
3	5	7
8	1	6

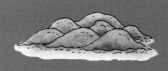

North east
The element of Earth
Education

This part of the house rules study, reflection, new ideas, knowledge, information and education. If you need a study or a place to sit and think, this is it. You can use darker colours here and a bright light will offset any gloom. It would be a good idea to try to turn this into a peaceful corner where you can curl up in an armchair and do some reading or thinking whenever you feel the urge. Alternatively, put your library of books and your computer here, especially if you use CD Rom and the Internet to find information. Earthenware pots or a fascinating piece of crystal on a shelf here will also help. This area represents new ideas and also new interests or novelty coming into your life, so if you don't want to stagnate mentally you should give yourself space to unwind and to think.

4	9	2
3	5	7
8	1	6

South
The element of Fire
Fame, recognition, reputation

This Square rules fame and recognition, also your reputation and how you are viewed or respected by others. You may not wish to be famous but you will enjoy being well thought of and we all need status in whatever society we live in. If you neglect this area, you will find your self-esteem taking a knock. This sector is dedicated to the element of Fire so a fireplace would be nice here. It doesn't matter whether the fire is wood burning or whether it uses coal, gas or electricity but a gas or electric fire will work better from the Feng Shui point of view if it has a flame effect. If this is impossible, a bright object or a brightly coloured picture will do the trick.

4	9	2
3	5	7
8	1	6

The Hall or Passage

Key West in Florida in America is a fascinating holiday area and if you ever have the luck to visit there and to take the guided bus tour around the island, your guide will point out several examples of tiny wooden "shot-gun" houses. These small Victorian structures were built with a central passage that started at the front door and ended at the back door. The idea was that in very hot weather, both doors could be left open to encourage a breeze through the home. The quaint name "shot-gun" houses, came from the fact that one could theoretically stand in the front garden and shoot straight through into the back garden without damaging the house. Well... so the story goes.

The Chinese believe that fast moving Sha Chi or even fast moving evil spirits are encouraged by such an in-line passage-way and they suggests that nothing but bad luck could ever come of living in such a house. If you happen to live in a house that has both the front and back doors in-line or if your hallway is long and straight, you must break the pattern in some way. You could place a semi-circular table half way up the hall or use an old-fashioned coat and hat stand to displace and slow the flow of Chi. Dangle a small wind chime in the hall or attach a flute over the doors to break up the Sha Chi and to encourage something far better. (The Cantonese like flutes because in their language the word flute sounds like the word "disappear"). A carpet or rugs on the floor with a mild pattern, perhaps a slightly wavy or swirly one will also help. Whatever shape your hallway is, you should paint it a light colour and ensure that there is plenty of light to see by especially where there are stairs to be climbed. Never put a mirror at the top or the bottom of the stairs, because apart from encouraging poor Chi, this is disorientating and dangerous.

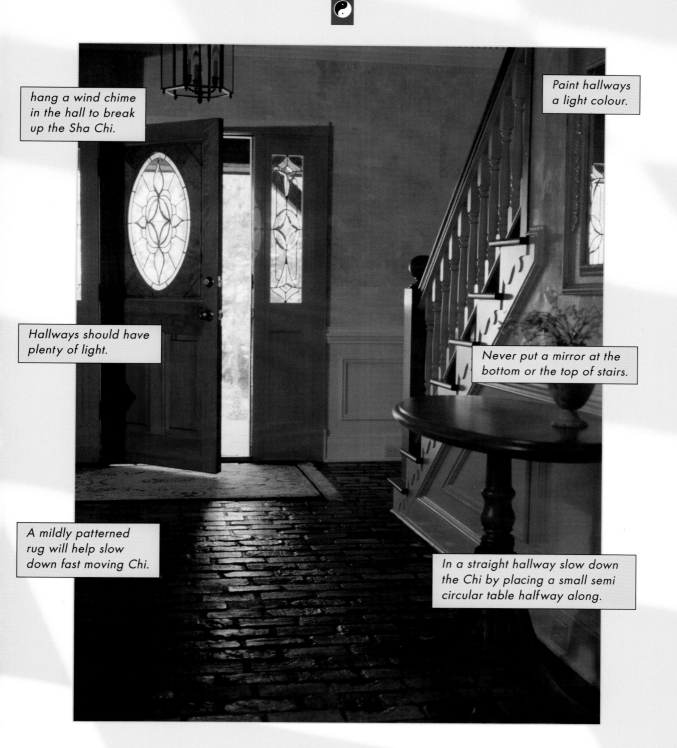

hang a wind chime in the hall to break up the Sha Chi.

Paint hallways a light colour.

Hallways should have plenty of light.

Never put a mirror at the bottom or the top of stairs.

A mildly patterned rug will help slow down fast moving Chi.

In a straight hallway slow down the Chi by placing a small semi circular table halfway along.

The rules of Feng Shui state that a solid front door with or without a small glass panel, is fine while a door that is completely made of glass is not. However, a glass back door or a glass panel in the back door is said to be favourable, and if opens out into a pleasant terrace or lawn, so much the better. A back door should not open on to a view of a garage or shed or a large tree as this will distract auspicious Chi. If the hallway is dark and cramped a good trick is to change any solid internal doors for glass ones and enhance the situation even more by putting a mirror on the wall that faces the door, so that the pleasant room is reflected in the mirror.

A nice idea is to put a picture of a tiger or one of those David Shepherd lion or elephant prints facing towards the front door as this will also help chase bad influences out of the home.

A curved staircase or one that turns is liked while a straight one is not. You can slow the movement of Chi up and down a straight staircase by hanging up a wind-chime or placing a heavy umbrella stand at the bottom. A pottery umbrella stand or a statue can also be placed in the corner of a half-landing to encourage the Chi to move slowly around it.

A front door completely made of glass is not good Feng Shui. Doors should be solid or just have a small glass panel.

A curved staircase is preferable to a straight one.

Windows

Windows should be functional, that is double glazed to keep the house warm in winter but so that they can be opened to bring in cool breezes in hot weather. Windows should be shaded with blinds or curtains when the sun is too strong. Everybody likes a nice view and it is good Feng Shui too. If a window faces a blank wall, train shrubs and flowers up this or paint a mural on the wall – or both. If you have a shelf inside a kitchen window that has no real view, place some pot plants on this to improve its aspect. If the corner of a building or a sharp pole or pylon faces a window or the back door, you can divert the secret arrows that are thrown towards the house by putting a tiny mirror on the door or window, facing this outwards to deflect the arrow.

Place pot plants on a window ledge where there is no view to improve the aspect.

Windows should shaded with blinds or curtains when the sun is too strong.

Windows should be functional so that they may be opened in hot weather and well sealed in cold weather.

A pretty view out of a window is a major component to the Feng Shui in a room.

Rounded tables living plants and fresh flowers break up the squared shapes in this room.

The Elements

Before we go any further we must look at the concept of the five elements. In Chinese astrology and in all other forms of divination, the elements are known as the Heavenly Stems, while the twelve signs of the Chinese zodiac – the Rat, Ox, Tiger etc. are known as the Earthly Branches. Feng Shui uses the concept of the elements quite extensively but the animal signs of the Earthly Branches which are also on the Chinese compass (the Lo Pan) only enter into Feng Shui at a much higher level than we can cope with in this book.

The five elements are Wood, Fire, Earth, Metal and Water and each relates to an area on the Pa Kua or Magic Circle.

If one element is found in an area, in order to enhance the feng shui in this area you must add the element which follows it in the cycle. In order to enhance the area you must ad the element which produces it. This list is in the correct order and according to the Chinese, when they are used in this order each element enhances the next. This is called the creative cycle.

The creative cycle

Wood burns to create Fire.

Fire creates ashes which return to the Earth.

Earth is compressed and metal is formed.

Metal is found in the Earth's veins.

Water springs from these veins and irrigates Wood.

The ancients believed that the Metal element that hid in the Earths veins, from these produce springs and underground rivers. Let us not argue with the incorrect physics but simply take the system on board as it stands.

If you view the list of elements in the creative cycle, those that are two elements apart are said to be destructive to each other. The illustrations will show you what I mean.

Wood (1) and Earth (3) are incompatible.

Earth (3) and Water (5) are incompatible.

Water (5) and Fire (2) are incompatible.

Fire (2) and Metal (4) are incompatible.

Metal (4) and Wood (1) are incompatible.

Using these elements together in areas will reduce or destroy the influence of an element in that particular area for instance if ....

In the destructive cycle:

Wood exhausts the Earth.

Earth pollutes the Water.

Water extinguishes Fire.

Fire Melts down the Metal.

Metal cuts and destroys Wood.

You can refer back to this chapter when we start to look at rooms and to see which elements can be used to remedy a poor situation.

The Kitchen

The Chinese take cooking and eating very seriously and they consider the kitchen to be the most important room in the house. A north facing kitchen is not considered good because the kitchen is associated with the element of Fire and the north is the Water direction. The kitchen must be clean and well ventilated and clear of unnecessary clutter.

If you turn back to the chapter on the Magic Square you will find your lucky number at the top of the column of birth dates. The Chinese take the stove or oven so seriously that they even link its direction with the cook's lucky number.

Lucky number	Best Direction for oven
1	East
2	West
3	North
4	South
5	West for a man, North West for a woman
6	North East
7	South West
8	North West
9	South East

Many people like to eat in their kitchen and it can also become a focus for everything that goes on in a family, but the Chinese take cooking and kitchens so seriously that they don't like this idea at all. I know myself that cooking requires concentration and if I don't have a modicum of peace in which to prepare a meal, I will not only make a mess of it but I am sure to end up cutting or burning myself into the bargain. It is not easy to prepare a meal in a place where the phone is claiming your attention and where children and pets run in and out or take up residence. You may not fancy the idea of having a kitchen that is isolated from the activities in the house, but if you are going to do anything more than simply rip the top from a supermarket meal, you will need a calm and traffic free place in which to work.

A toilet that leads off from the kitchen must be separated from it by two doors. This is not only good Feng Shui but is also a building regulation. The Chinese consider toilets very dirty and they don't like them anywhere near kitchens. If a little sink can be included in the space between the toilet door and the kitchen door, so much the better.

NB: A personal comment. I have travelled a great deal in the Orient and I have eaten some really strange meals while there but I have never gone down with tummy trouble, so either I have a very strong stomach or the Chinese truly adhere to the rules of Feng Shui. Perhaps I have been lucky, but I have never come across a dirty toilet either in mainland China or in any other place that the Chinese inhabit.

It is considered bad luck to have a kitchen door that is in a direct line with the front or the back door. If it is in line with both of these, as is often the case in Victorian terrace houses in Britain, this will result in increasing illness and loss of money in the household. Either keep the doors shut of if that is impractical, hang a plant up somewhere in order to break up the flow of Chi. If you can put your hands on a gold coloured bowl, place this somewhere in your kitchen, and perhaps keep a little rice in the bowl for good luck.

Some traditions consider it to be good Feng Shui to place the oven facing a door that leads into the rest of the house, because this will bring a feeling of warmth and comfort into the house. Other traditions don't like this idea because it means that the cook will have to work with his or her back to a doorway where passers by can't be seen and where a knife-wielding enemy could creep up on one. However, wherever your oven is, it should not be adjacent to a sink or the fridge as these are ruled by the element of Water while the oven naturally comes under the element of Fire. An oven, sink or work surface that is placed in such a way that the cook has to work with his back to a door can be improved by hanging up a small mirror so that the cook can see what is going on behind him.

The oven or stove shouldn't be directly beneath a skylight as this will dissipate the good Chi from your cooking straight up through the roof. Anything as important as a stove, sink or work surface should not be placed directly under a beam or rolled steel joist. If this can't be helped, perhaps hang some kitchen equipment or decorative items such as a collection of jugs from this so as to break up the heavy Chi. If you don't want to lose money, keep the top of your stove or oven clean.

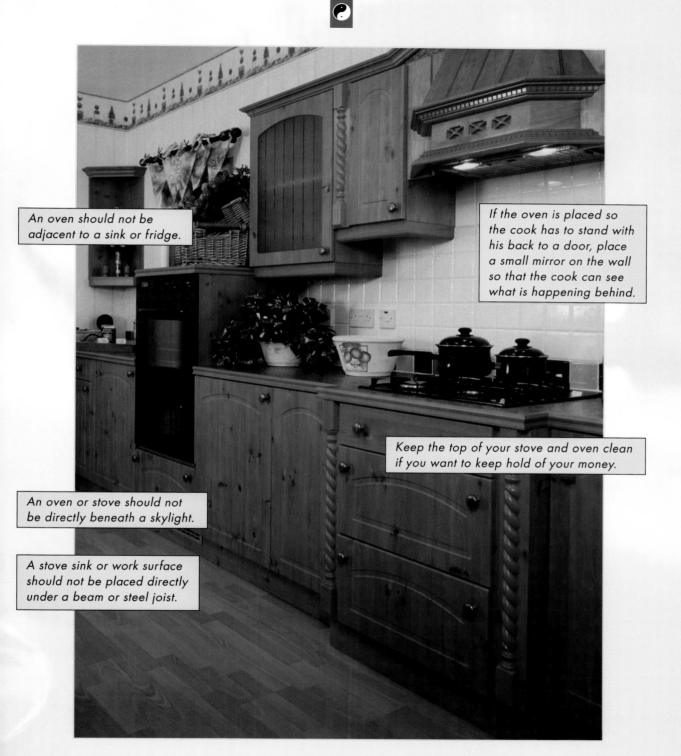

An oven should not be adjacent to a sink or fridge.

If the oven is placed so the cook has to stand with his back to a door, place a small mirror on the wall so that the cook can see what is happening behind.

Keep the top of your stove and oven clean if you want to keep hold of your money.

An oven or stove should not be directly beneath a skylight.

A stove sink or work surface should not be placed directly under a beam or steel joist.

A small and functional kitchen is pretty much all Fire and Water. The element that links both Fire and Water is Wood, so either put wooden doors on the kitchen cupboards or add some wood by introducing a wooden bread-bin, a wooden salad bowl or a wooden cup filled with wooden spoons. Woody plants or a bonsai tree might be a good thing to have on the windowsill. If your oven faces your sink they will fight each other! The way to prevent this is to use some green on the floor between them or to hang a green teacloth on the oven door.

Never put cutlery in a drawer in a dead corner as this will encourage stagnant Chi to land up on your dinner table and causing disharmony in the family and possibly also indigestion!

Add wood to your fire and water environment in the kitchen by placing woody plants on the windowsill.

If your oven faces your sink, put something green between them either on the floor or hang a green teacloth on the oven door.

Never put cutlery in a drawer in a dead corner as this will result in stagnant Chi being served up at your meal table.

Introduce wood into your kitchen by adding wooden doors or a wooden work surface as in this case.

The Dining Area

A window that faces east or west is a great help in stimulating good Chi in this room. Ideally, a dining table should be oval or round with no hard edged corners. A rounded table symbolises heaven while a square or rectangular one is related to the earth. A table that has sharp corners will throw secret arrows all round the room. Put the table in the centre of the room so that all the family can sit around it and then adhere to the Chinese style of placing the family.

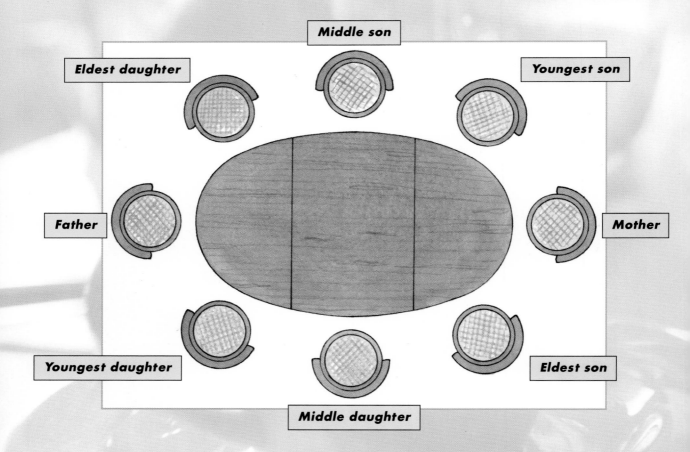

If you don't have a separate dining room, try to section off this part of the room with a screen or some furniture or an arrangement of plants.

It is better Feng Shui to eat by a good light rather than by candle light. Of course, candles can be put on the table, but the diners should be able to see what they are eating. The décor should be fairly plain and it should not distract from the serious business of eating. Family gatherings and conversation around the table are to be encouraged but sitting with a tray on one's lap and shovelling down food while

The Chinese prefer an even number of chairs around a dining table.

The decor in a dining room should be fairly plain and not detract from the serious business of eating.

Chairs should be comfortable with good backs and preferably with arms.

watching the television is definitely not the Chinese way. My own extended family is from all over Europe and we all take eating very seriously, and we like sitting at the table and enjoying our meal while talking over the day's news with each other.

The Chinese prefer an even number of chairs at the dining table as the odd one out is likely to feel lonely. Chairs should be comfortable with good backs and preferably also with arms, but chairs with arms are not easy to find in the UK or elsewhere in the west, so you will probably have to put up with less than perfect Feng Shui here. Try to avoid placing diners with their backs to windows or doorways if at all possible. If dining in the evening in a small room, draw the curtains as this will make the diners feel cosy and secure. Never sit with your own back to the door.

The colours that you use in your dining room can promote a healthy atmosphere for digestion. Reds and yellows are excellent for stimulating the appetite and for digestion but if your appetite needs no further stimulation, swap the red for pink, coral or peach and bright yellow for pale lemon or a shade of mustard. Pale blue and green are also great as is lavender. Orange will make the diners feel sick and is only a good choice if you are landed with unwelcome visitors who you want to chase out of your home!

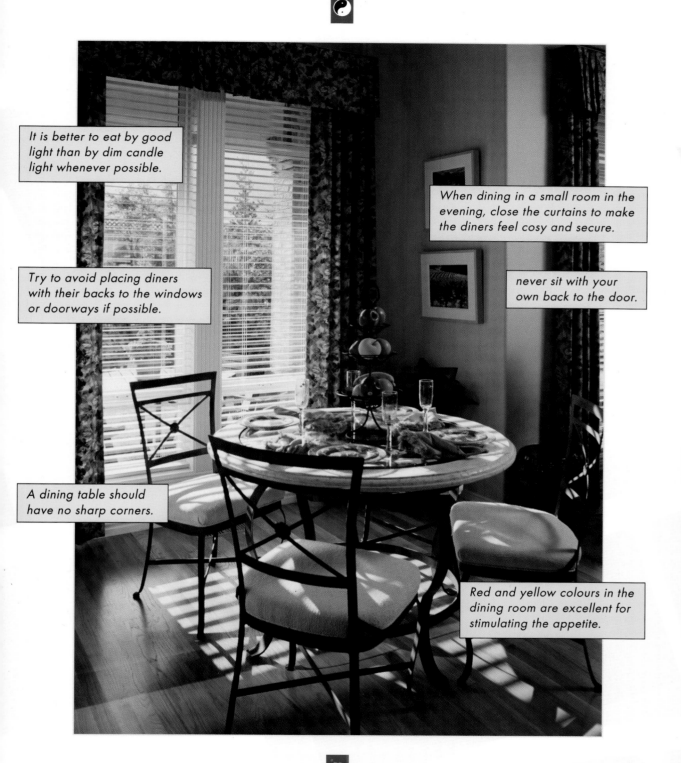

It is better to eat by good light than by dim candle light whenever possible.

When dining in a small room in the evening, close the curtains to make the diners feel cosy and secure.

Try to avoid placing diners with their backs to the windows or doorways if possible.

never sit with your own back to the door.

A dining table should have no sharp corners.

Red and yellow colours in the dining room are excellent for stimulating the appetite.

The Living Room

During the period of time that I have spent writing this book, there has been a fascinating television series running that is called "The House Doctor". The basis of the programme is that someone who is having trouble selling their home calls in a pleasant American lady who advises them on how to improve their home in order to make it sell. Many of her tips align perfectly with Feng Shui. One of these is to make a fireplace the focus of the living room rather than having a large television and/or a collection of hi-fi equipment dominating the room. Feng Shui agrees totally with this. If you can keep your television to one side and minimise the effect of hi-fi and other stuff, the room will feel far more welcoming. Such equipment, along with computer equipment is a mixture of the elements of Metal and Water and while a little of these is wonderful, too much of them dominating the room is not good.

Televisions and hi-fi equipment should not dominate the living room and should be screened off and hidden whenever they are not in use.

A nice square or rectangular living room is best as there is nowhere for Chi to collect and stagnate. Unless your room is very small, avoid pushing the furniture against the walls so that it ends up looking like a dentist's waiting room, but arrange your seating in a horseshoe formation so that everybody can feel comfortable.

If your living room is not rectangular but an odd shape, put a plant in the odd shaped end in order to liven it up and to prevent stale Chi from gathering. Try to avoid sitting with your back to the door as this will make you feel insecure.

This is where you can use the Magic Square once again to maximise the potential for happiness in family and social life. This time, place your Magic Square over the living room with the side marked 8,1,6 on the side where people usually enter the room.

The areas that you want to emphasise in this room are:

Sector 2 Relationships

Sector 3 Family

Sector 6 Friends

Sector 7 Children

A nice square or rectangular living room is best where there is no room for stagnant Chi to collect.

Use a mirror over a fireplace which has been blocked off to make a small room seem more spacious.

Avoid placing seats under a beam as this will make the occupant insecure.

Furniture size and shape should be in-keeping with the room.

Avoid putting seats under a beam as this will induce insecurity in those who sit there. Use the less importantly numbered areas of your room for sideboards, shelving, plants and other "fillers". Try to keep the centre of this room and the dining table tidy, if you have one, because this is a considered to be a minor health area which will encourage well-being if it is kept clear of clutter and mess. Your furniture should be in keeping with the size and shape of the room. Cushions and soft furnishings will soften the room and introduce a touch of feminine Yin into a heavily masculine room. Flowers and plants will encourage good Chi and they will soften any secret arrows that are in the room. It is considered inauspicious to use dried flowers and any cut flowers should be thrown out before they start to die.

Mirrors are useful when you need to extend an area of the house but avoid placing a mirror in such a way that the reflection cuts your head in half when you are seated. A mirror over a fireplace as this is said to encourage good Chi to vanish up the chimney, but if the fireplace is ornamental and not actually used as an open fire, this is fair enough and a mirror over the fireplace can make a small room feel larger or brighter. Finally, a tank of fish is considered a wonderful thing for promoting luck, money, harmony and peace. If your living room is situated at the front of the house, this is definitely a great place to have one.

Do not use any dried flowers and replace or remove fresh flowers before they die.

Bedrooms

It is best for a bedroom only to be used for sleeping in and for changing your clothes. A bedroom that has a double purpose such as part-time study or office won't promote a good night's sleep. If you have no option but to use it in this way, try to separate the work area from the sleeping area and use a screen to hide any work stuff away. Keep computers and televisions out of the bedroom if at all possible but if you must have a television there, at least keep it away from the foot of the bed. It would be nice to have a view of trees from your bedroom window but if this is not possible, treat yourself to a pretty picture to give you something nice to look at.

One thing that all Feng Shui experts are absolutely agreed upon is that it is inauspicious for your bedroom door to face your toilet door. If this is unavoidable, use tiny mirror on the outside of the toilet door to reflect good Chi back into the bedroom. Close the doors and if you can remember to do so, keep your toilet seat down. If the toilet is in full view, your sleeping pattern will be disturbed and worse still, your sex life and your marriage could "go down the toilet".

These days we all love the idea of an ensuite bathroom but if you have one of these, remember to shut the door and put the toilet lid down. Such a bathroom can drain energy from the bedroom, as would placing the bed directly beneath a skylight.

Never place a bed beneath a beam as this is said to promote poor health and disturbed nights. If you have absolutely no choice, then fix some kind of rail effect beneath the beam and drape soft fabric around it to break up the beam's weighty feel. There are rules about exactly where you place a bed but in many houses there isn't enough room to make a choice. Avoid sleeping under a heavy light fitting or a

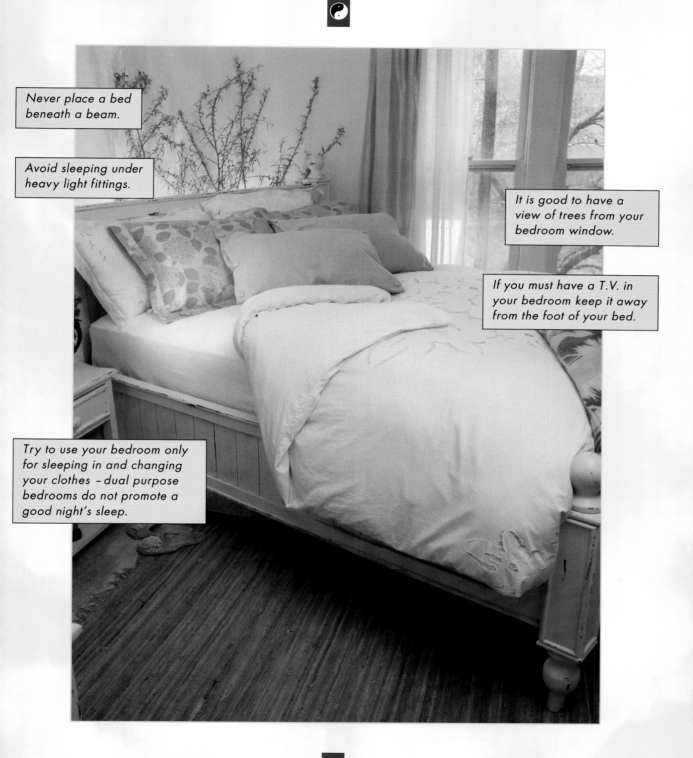

Never place a bed beneath a beam.

Avoid sleeping under heavy light fittings.

It is good to have a view of trees from your bedroom window.

If you must have a T.V. in your bedroom keep it away from the foot of your bed.

Try to use your bedroom only for sleeping in and changing your clothes – dual purpose bedrooms do not promote a good night's sleep.

Avoid placing mirrors opposite the bed

Place your bed in the highest point of the room and never beneath the slope of a ceiling as in this case chandelier. In a case where the electricity supply to your light is directly above the bed, you can use a trick that I picked up in the USA. Screw a hook in the ceiling in the place where you would like your light fitting to hang, and use a decorative chain with a matching flex wound around it to link the place where the cord enters the ceiling to the place where you want your light to hang. If you sleep in an attic, place the bed in the highest point of the room rather than under the slope of the ceiling.

If you can choose the position of your bed, ensure that the back of it is against a wall. You should avoid sleeping with the head of the bed against a window, as this will make you feel unsafe. Don't jam the foot of the bed against a wall as this will make the occupant of the bed feel claustrophobic. The Chinese don't like a bed that is placed directly opposite a door, because dead bodies are taken out feet first and they don't want to be reminded of this while climbing into bed. (Oddly enough, this is superstition is shared by the Jews).

The Chinese believe that the soul leaves the body and goes on astral journeys while we sleep and if the returning soul sees a large mirror opposite the bed with the sleeper reflected in it, it might lose its way and try to enter the mirror rather than coming back to the sleeping person. A dressing table mirror should not oppose the window as the glare from outside will be reflected in it. Furniture should not be placed around the bed in an arc as this will lower the health and vitality of the sleeper.

Sharp corners are said to shoot secret arrows, so try to avoid sleeping directly in line with one of these. However, too many curved edges encourages the Chi to swirl around too rapidly, so a balance should be struck here. Metal bedsteads can shoot secret arrows at a sleeper, as can the posts in four poster beds, but these can be soften with draped muslin or chiffon.

Ensure that the back of the bed is against a wall

Soften the posts on four poster beds by draping chiffon or muslin over them.

Do not jam the foot of the bed against a wall.

Do not place the foot of a bed opposite a door.

Children's bedrooms

The east or south east are the most propitious directions for children's bedrooms. The Chinese see the east as the place of the rising sun and the direction from which springtime comes. This optimistic outlook promotes growth and health. The east is associated with the element of Wood which is also attuned to curiosity and idealism. The south is brings the fruitfulness of summer and the link between this and the element of Fire encourages intellect and energy but too much energy can cause aggression, so a south-east placement is auspicious. If you happen to live in the southern hemisphere, the north east would be a better placement.

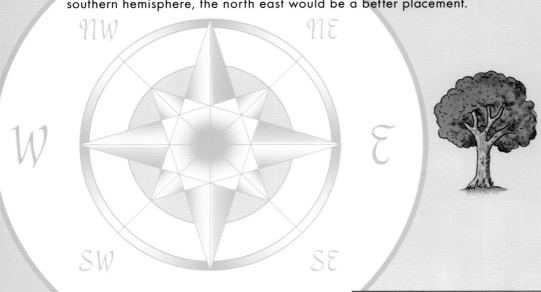

The most propitious direction for children's bedrooms in the Northern Hemisphere is the South East. In the Southern Hemisphere the North East would be a better placement.

The room should be rectangular or square and it should have adequate ventilation and light. Young children need to be close to their parents. Try to keep toys and mess away from the centre of a child's room to ensure continued good health.

Green is a good colour choice as this is also associated with spring and the eastern direction, but blue will calm down an overactive or aggressive child while red or even pink will enliven a shy or withdrawn one.

Pink or red in a bedroom will enliven a shy or withdrawn child.

Blue will calm down an overactive or aggressive child.

The Bathroom and Toilet Suite

The best direction for the bathroom and toilet is the north because this is considered to be a good place for private matters and time spent alone. The north is also aligned with the element of Water and this obviously links well with a bathroom. The worst is the south east because this is where money can drain away. It is also a good idea to position the bathroom at the back of the house where it can have no effect on important matters such as family life, health or wealth.

Water colours are black and blue, so in theory these are good colours to choose. However, this might give the bathroom too much of the Yin element that is associated with water. Perhaps a supporting element such as Metal or Wood can be introduced. Metal is associated with the colours white and grey and also with gold or silver metallic objects, and the shape associated with this element is an oval. A purist would choose a white bath, sink and toilet, an oval rug in any colour other than red or yellow and metal fixtures. Wood is also helpful, as is the colour green.

Keep the bathroom and toilet doors closed if you don't want your money to fall down the drain. If it is possible to train your family to keep the lid on the toilet seat down, do so. If your bathroom is not in an ideal position in your house, things can be helped by fixing a small decorated mirror in the door that faces out into the hall, bedroom or wherever, this will throw the good Chi back into the house.

Fix all leaky taps if you don't want your strength and financial resources to drain away. If there is no natural light, fix plenty of mirrors on the walls. Ensure that mirrors are plain and not divided up so that they have the effect of dividing your face into sections. Keep mirrors clean. A ventilation device could drain Chi from the bathroom, but you may have to use one and live with this small loss. Living plants are a good aid to encouraging the gentle movement of beneficial Chi. As this room is so Yin in nature, it might be an idea to introduce a little Yang by having a few candles standing around.

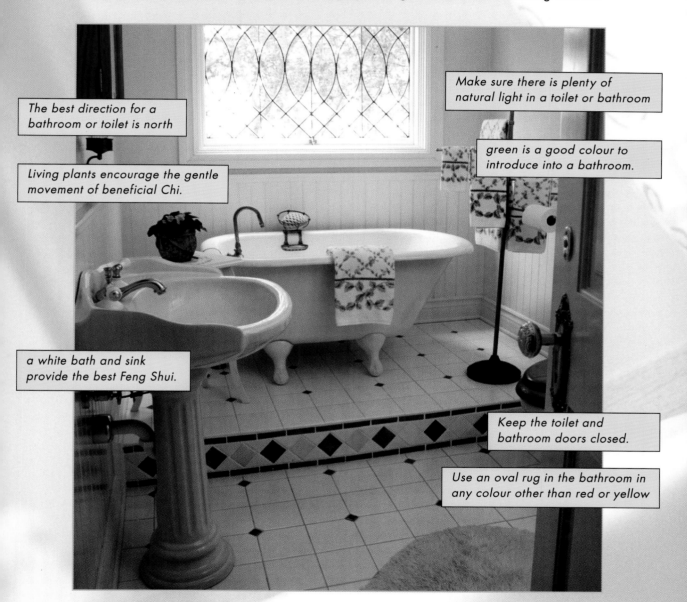

The best direction for a bathroom or toilet is north

Make sure there is plenty of natural light in a toilet or bathroom

Living plants encourage the gentle movement of beneficial Chi.

green is a good colour to introduce into a bathroom.

a white bath and sink provide the best Feng Shui.

Keep the toilet and bathroom doors closed.

Use an oval rug in the bathroom in any colour other than red or yellow

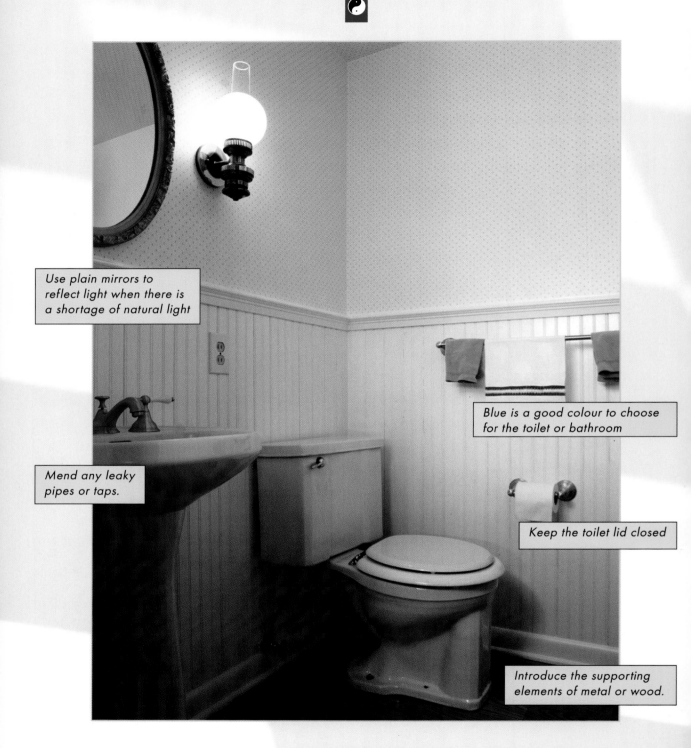

Use plain mirrors to reflect light when there is a shortage of natural light

Mend any leaky pipes or taps.

Blue is a good colour to choose for the toilet or bathroom

Keep the toilet lid closed

Introduce the supporting elements of metal or wood.

A Single Living Space

A bed-sitting room needs to be kept tidy and the centre (health) area kept clear of dirty mugs, piles of papers and mess. Divide up the space into separate areas for sleeping and living if and possible screen off any area that you use for writing or working in. You might be able to utilise the "leg" of an L-shaped end for a bed or futon.

Choose curved or rounded furniture in the area where you sleep, eat and live, also soften a particularly sharp looking chair with a "throw" or use plants to break up the image. Sharp square pieces are great for an area in which you study or work but you must take care not to have a really sharp corner pointing at your bed. A pot plant in a shiny metal container will do much to shoot back offending secret arrows.

Finally...

Now that you have read this book and arranged your house to the "nth" degree, make a start on the companion book and have a go at sorting out your garden.

Index

Index